THE NUDGE TO WRITE

VOLUME 1 — AN ANTHOLOGY

FIND & AMPLIFY YOUR VOICE
WRITING & SELF-PUBLISHING WORKSHOP

HOSTED BY SYDNEY JACKSON-CLOCKSTON & TAMARA CRIBLEY
CONTRIBUTORS TONYA ROCHE & KENT DESLONGCHAMP

Print ISBN: 978-1-961870-02-4
eBook ISBN: 978-1-961870-06-2

Library of Congress Control Number

Cover & Interior Designed by The Deliberate Page, LLC.

Printed in the United States of America
www.DeliberatePage.com

TABLE OF CONTENTS

INTRODUCTION 1

MEET THE HOSTS 3

The Nudge to Write 5

MY NUDGE TO WRITE: COLLECTION OF SHORT
INSPIRATIONAL WORKS 7
   BY KENT DESLONGCHAMP

MY NUDGE TO WRITE: IN THE BEGINNING... 29
   BY TONYA ROCHE

Writing Prompts 45

NOSTALGIC BITES 47
   WRITING PROMPT. 47

   HAM POT PIE - THE PENNSYLVANIA DUTCH WAY 49

   KENT'S COLLECTIVE CRAZY COLORFUL CHRISTMAS COOKIE AND
   CANDY CELEBRATION AND COLLABORATION STORY 51

   SESAME CHICKEN AND MY GRANDMOTHER 55

   "KAMABOKO?". 57

BUYING A NEW CAR. 59

   MOOD AND TONE WRITING EXERCISE 59

CHOOSE YOUR OWN PROMPT. 67

   WE ARE GOING TO PARTY LIKE IT'S 1999 71

   THE DOOR IN THE FLOOR 77

   WHO AM I? WHO AM I MEANT TO BE? 79

   IT'S LIKE A RALLY CROSS COARSE…. 83

AN INVITATION TO FIND & AMPLIFY *YOUR* VOICE 87

INTRODUCTION

Welcome to *The Nudge to Write: Volume One*. This book stemmed from a question asked during a conversation between myself and Tamara Cribley, owner and founder of The Deliberate Page. I'm not sure who brought the question up first, but the question was, "How can we make the writing process less confusing and the steps to self-publishing more equitable?."

As a neurodiverse author myself who fumbled my way through the writing, editing, formatting, copyediting, self-publishing, and marketing processes of becoming a self-published author, I know firsthand how insurmountable it can be to get from point A to point Z. Especially if you don't have oodles of money to pay for support through each step. This is why Tamara and I wanted to create a workshop series that was both affordable and walked folks through the process of becoming a published author.

When meeting in preparation for our workshop series Tamara and I both challenged ourselves to think about how we could dig deeper and truly make the largest positive impact on writers both in our workshop and aspiring writers outside of our workshop as well. This intentionality led to the birth of the book you are now reading.

It's our belief that anyone who wants to write and self-publish can, if given the opportunity. This book was our way of not just lecturing in our workshop on the mechanics of writing and self-publishing, but this book serves as a way to intentionally create space, showing workshop participants how to navigate the process. Throughout this book, you are going to see excerpts from each workshop participant on their journey to becoming a published writer. Each contribution will provide you with a narrative that hopefully inspires you to get started on your own writing journey or empowers you to follow a passion project of your own. We also included sample prompts from our writing workshop so you can see firsthand some of the exercises we went through to support writers in finding their unique voices.

So if you are reading this, here before you is proof that our vision was a success. Tamara and I both want to congratulate the new authors of this book! Cheers to publishing the first of many. We also want to congratulate you, the reader, on becoming a part of our community. Whether you plan to start writing yourself or just love supporting independent authors by reading their work, your reading this book is a reason to celebrate.

Passion Over Perfection,

Sydney Jackson-Clockston
Owner and Founder
Citrine Unlimited LLC.
Stardust and Co Publishing LLC.

MEET THE HOSTS

The *Find & Amplify Your Voice Writing and Self-Publishing Workshop Series* is a collaboration between Tamara Cribley of The Deliberate Page, and Sydney Jackson-Clockston of Citrine Unlimited. Each brings her own unique experiences and knowledge to share. Together, they bring you a comprehensive experience that will help you successfully write and publish your very own book.

 With over twenty years of experience in marketing and design, Tamara has spent the last decade serving independent authors and helping them to successfully publish professional-quality books for print and digital platforms. She has written and published over two dozen articles on the topic of professionalism in self-publishing.

Connect with Tamara:
Tamara@DeliberatePage.com
Website: www.DeliberatePage.com
Facebook: www.facebook.com/DeliberatePage
LinkedIn: www.linkedin.com/in/Cribley

Sydney is a 2022 Good Business Colorado Award recipient known for her impactful Leadership Development Coaching style and ability to create custom trainings and workshops for various organizations. She is the author of *My Own Worst*
Enemy: Understanding and Overcoming Imposter Syndrome and a contributor in the anthology *The Badass Within: Stories of Strength, Hope and Courage.* As a writer with dyslexia, Sydney understands what it's like to have the desire to write but still struggle with the confidence and direction to get started. She loves supporting others to push past their inner critic and take the plunge into achieving their authorship dreams.

Connect with Sydney:
hello@citrineunlimited
Website: www.citrineunlimited.com
Facebook: www.facebook.com/sydstarr
LinkedIn: www.linkedin.com/in/sydneyjc

THE NUDGE TO
Write

IN THEIR OWN WORDS

The following essays are in various states of 'finished.' Some are relatively polished, while others are in the earliest stages of writing and development. The goal of each exercise was to explore different ways to express voice and intent. As such, the majority of these writings have been through limited editing and revision. We invite you to experience the writing of Kent Deslongchamp and Tonya Roche, along with prompts by hosts Tamara Cribley and Sydney Jackson-Clockston.

MY NUDGE TO WRITE: COLLECTION OF SHORT INSPIRATIONAL WORKS

BY KENT DESLONGCHAMP

THE JOURNEY

What you are about to read are my unique takeaways and insights, based upon the comprehensive and incredulous experiences, shared adventures, and the participation in, *The Find & Amplify Your Voice Workshop Series* and *Find Your Voice Writing Workshop.* The journey entailed a maze of complexities intertwined in a variety of challenging elements. By pushing through my doubts, fears, and ambivalences, in discovering and embracing my writing styles, genres, and brands and the building upon inspirations, connections, and passions, the amazing achievement, accomplishment, and my life-long personal dream, authorship, and publication of my own book, was at last fulfilled and the objective of the workshop was attained with complete satisfaction.

THE WORK

Every story starts somewhere; it has a beginning marked by a moment in time when all that has been stagnated and sedentary begins to stir. This movement is a catalyst to spark energy, to ignite power, to awaken the soul, and bring the story to life. This is my beginning, each of you, the catalyst, sparking my energy, giving me the power needed to rejuvenate and awaken my soul, bringing life into the ink, and the momentum building with each word penned, the magnitude growing with each sentence. Each sentence enticing desire in the vested interest in how the story unfolds, and the aspiration in reaching the final outcome, achieving the desired goal, the completion of the written story.

FIND YOUR VOICE

My initial thought, when I read the title of the workshop *Find your Voice*, was that I had no interest. My voice is not one of my attributes that needs to be found. My voice is always heard, it is loud, boisterous, rambunctious, ostentatious, and direct. Friends have joked that my voice is so loud, it could be used as a beacon and homing device to locate someone lost; anywhere, anytime, and in any place.

AMPLIFY YOUR VOICE

The second workshop, *Amplify your Voice*, was equally unattractive and I thought unneeded. My voice is not only marked by intensity to volume or level of sound, but may be heard as vehement, intrusive, tactless, and brash and my nature seen as disdainful, disrespectful, egotistical, and arrogant. Finding your voice, I learned, is a process—a means of discovery. It involves measuring your intent and understanding the impact of reception. It means learning to communicate clearly and effectively, using the right tone, precise words, active listening, and interactive communication. Finding your voice also means ensuring that the other party understands you—the same transcending indifference. To find your voice is to be aware, alert, and alive, to amplify your call to action.

Being amplified means requiring focus and precision. It means that each word matters, each word thoughtful and measured. It means seeing both sides of the coin and applying these perceptions to make informed choices, allowing for learned decisions to be formed, and resulting in balanced outcomes. To amplify your voice means that even at the lowest volume with the minimal words and the use of a neutral tone, your impact can be profound. To amplify your voice is the means to fulfill, accomplish, and resonate your call to action.

BREATHE

As air is fundamental to breathing and breathing essential to life, so are thoughts and ideas fundamental to writing, and words essential to breathe life into thoughts and ideas. This creative process sets in motion the ebb and flow of writing, the essence created by the melding of words and ideas. Storyboarding is the method I choose to achieve this creative process. I write down anything, everything, and all things that come into my mind. Next, I rearrange the words into sub-circles. I focus on two or three of the circles that resonate with a connection, evoke a strong emotion, or that I find influential or empowering. I then begin to bring together these ideas, narrow them down, make them more precise and redefine them. This sets into place a focal point from which to expand upon the formation of each idea, leading to a thesis filled with supportive content enriched with details that segue from page to page, building upon each other. The compilation of these completed processes is the final step, to achieve the end result and accomplish the desired outcome, a written work of art that you possess in your mind, your heart, and your soul, to hold and have, to revisit as often as you want and to carry with you forever and always.

THE INTRODUCTION

It began on a warm winter Saturday morning. The 35-minute highway drive, which Google Maps had displayed as the fastest route to get from my home in Commerce City to the Hampden Library part of the Denver Public Library System, was painless and pleasant. I pulled into the small parking lot, filled with anticipatory energy and excitement. As I stepped out of my car, I heard Sydney's familiar and ever-welcoming voice calling my name. Then she opened her arms, the gesture implying the offering of a hug. I eagerly accepted this offering, both of us wrapping our arms, and then embracing in a genuine, heartfelt hug.

I was introduced to Tamara next, the co-host, who implied the same gesture, which was gladly accepted and we too wrapped our arms around each other and embraced in the same genuine and heartfelt hug. With the introductions completed, we marked the milestone of the first steps of the processes for the weekend writing workshop: complete. The meeting and greeting of my fellow student Tonya followed next. The same open armed gesture implying a hug, was also accepted as was the embrace and sharing of a genuine and heartfelt hug. With the scene now set, the mood established, the four of us embarked upon a most magnificent two-day adventure, which led me into unprecedented territory and beyond anything I had imagined. It was a *carpe diem* moment!

THE PROCESS

Within a matter of minutes, writing assignments were given, to be completed in a timed 15-minute period. It was the first challenge of many which set the stage for the workshop. The writing exercises were catalysts in forging my brain in preparation, setting it into place, initiating, thinking, and processing in writing mode. Writing mode requires both sides of the brain.

The left side of the brain allows for cognitive thinking, which is used for compilations, logic, theories, mathematical equations, data input, and critical decision-making, the processes done in a linear, step-by-step, sequential, systematic, and methodical fashion.

The right brain allows for creative and innovative thinking, sensory perception, and imagination. Which is instilled into our soul, through visualization, rhythms, and emotional responses; the processes enriched by color spectrums, beauty, nature, music, and aromas.

The assignments in class, along with the unexpected challenges and unforeseen complexities required both the left and the right brain to accomplish. Each side of the brain, shifting in order, taking priority, to apply the associated process necessary to complete each task, accomplishing the desired outcome and achieve the final goal successfully.

In a matter of 48 hours, I walked away with a newly acquired portfolio of knowledge and skill sets; a plethora of unprecedented personal experiences, and profound perspectives, bringing life into this truly transcendental moment filled with the positive, inspiring, motivational, and enriching experiences. It was well worth the time, money and effort, and 100% effective in reaching every goal and desired objective.

STATE OF BEING

It was time to begin the assignment. As always, step one for me is the process of putting my rambling thoughts into categories which resonate with clarity and focus upon the poignant ideas, emanating the right emotions to obtain the right frame of mind. Next, by lengthening the spine, softening the shoulders, and releasing tension, the muscles relax, procuring a calm, peaceful state of mind, enhancing soothing energy to forge ahead and begin a short story.

CREATIVE NONFICTION

The perplexing perspectives and complex core elements found in Creative Nonfiction, along with subgenre umbrellas Memoir, Personal Essay, Narrative History and Auto (Biographical) Fiction, glorify my own unique writing style and bring to life my literary endeavors. The essence of this genre pushes boundaries with imaginative exploration, delving into our deepest convictions, instilling intimate personal reflections, blurring the lines between fact and fiction. My core writings stem from the expressive exploratory and essential values found in Creative Nonfiction blending the imaginary with reality and indulging in the creation of fantastic fruition.

The genre also empowers the inspiration to entice, awaken and bring to life the transformative potential for my readers to pursue and divulge the depiction of their own stories, fulfill their deepest desires and their profound passions, embracing their own differences, navigating through real life via a vast array of enhanced dramatizations and securing, and setting into place, an opportunistic arena for creativity, in pursuit of their own written works and writing endeavors.

RESONATING WITH READERS

With such conviction in every sentence I craft, I aim to resonate with readers who identify themselves as LGBTQ+; those who struggle to be heard, to be seen, or to be recognized in a world that is fast paced, filled with filters, selective hearing, and tunnel vision. By giving vivid descriptions and creating strong-minded characters who challenge the system and question values, I give those struggling with identity and self-love a positive image to instill pride and acceptance. I believe that storytelling has the power to break through all adversity that we may encounter in life. It provokes empowerment and resolution to any struggle and creates a meaningful and universal connection between me, the author, and each person who reads my story.

My writing lies in the commitment to those who have been oppressed for their identity. It is driven by my own struggles with stereotypes, labels, false pretensions, and hate-filled moments. Through my work, I strive to give hope, to give knowledge, to give acceptance, and to offer love. The heart of my literary endeavors are values such as diversity, truth, compassion, integrity, peace, and happiness. Each story takes on some political, economic, or human concern that is prevalent at the time of the writing. Through the characters, plots, and themes, I create a complete story with the power to uplift, sound off, unify, and open eyes to their concerns. Through this, we can bring about change in ourselves, in each other, and in the world.

My writing is not just a craft, but me putting my heart, soul, and self out there for all to see. In this way, if one person finds whatever they need to begin to love, to be heard, to stand proud and find their voice, then for me, that written work served the purpose that I set. Because I chose to write in the style that I do and communicate in the way that I do, I am literally (all pun intended) changing the world one person at a time. I can think of no other creation on this earth that is solely mine, where my intent is shaped and affected solely from my input, and my impact influenced and affected solely from my actions. That is why I write, and that is why I embarked in this workshop to find my voice, and to amplify my voice, and resonate for all to hear. That is why I will write until my last day on this earth.

If there was a book of short stories, eternal entries, an anthology of endless volumes of our stories, our conclusions, a combination of our symphonic sentences, our moments of voices found and voices amplified, a mixed melodious menage mastered with the details of distinct, defined, minuscule moments of magnificence, combined and compiled to create a constituted collective self-story, uniquely construed memorializing us, our lives, our beliefs, our experiences, our moments, our journeys, and each of our stories together, a unified amplified voice telling our tales for all the cosmos to hear. *A Slice of Our Souls* - A Collection of Short Stories about the people that lived their incredulous lives on this lovely planet called Earth and their telling tales of their legacy and the making of this place that we call, our home.

This writing piece is based upon these three reasons to Why I Write and resonate my personal values and convictions, to Advocate, to Remember/Never Forget, and to Identify/Be Proud

What is Your Writing Goal? Reason 1 - Making a Difference, Reason 2 - Preserving Culture, Reason 3 - Exploring Identity

AVATAR – THE WAY OF THE GAY - I SEE YOU GIRL, PLEASE PUT SOME CLOTHES ON

In the movies *Avatar* & *Avatar – The Way of the Water* – "I See You," is the greeting that the Na'vi people of Pandora use to greet each other. It can be as simple as "hello", or a phrase used in show of respect and recognition when in the presence of someone in a position of power, the weak tribal members giving respected regard to the mighty, dissolving differences and unity emerging in its place. It can also mean more than seeing only the physical with your eyes. It can mean seeing *into* each other, a glimpse into the soul, understanding each other and embracing each other. It can be an expression of admiration. It is a recognition of one's true nature and soul. It can signify profound connection, despite differences, the communion in knowing that we are all connected. An understanding that our differences should be celebrated, accepting unity, the conceptual creed that until you see me, acknowledge me, I do not exist, and only when you see me, acknowledge me, do I materialize. Your recognition brings me into existence. This is the way of the gay - our connectedness is a premise that, indeed, we are all one, a rainbow of color, a collective identity, and a combined community. It is this philosophy, embodied with this belief, that this creation, this colorful character, represents the Kent Deslongchamp Avatar, and my influences, inspirations, values, and beliefs that collectively embrace my essences, all that I am and all that illuminates my existence.

This writing piece is based upon these 3 reasons Why I Write and resonate with my personal values and convictions, to Instill/ Legacy, to Never Stop Dreaming, and to Always Instill Fantasy Escape/Imagination

What is Your Writing Goal? Reason 1 – Creating a Legacy, Reason 2 – Pursuing and Fulfilling your Dreams, Reason – 3 Escaping Reality

EXTRA, EXTRA READ ALL ABOUT IT

"And now, high on top of the rooftop of Denver's premier and most desired place to be, the Fictitious and Fabulous Flamingo Fireside Restaurant, Lounge, and Cabaret. I am your host with the most, in all the right places, the daring and dashing Dan D Denver, along with the mesmerizing and always memorable Mimosa B Tasty, and the tantalizing and tempestuous Trio B Thropple. Yes, it is the momentous and monumental moment, the magnanimous event we all have anticipated and waited for, the unparalleled premier party. A presentation of the rad, reverend, renowned and raunchy, talk of the town, and most toasted talent of Denver, Kent Deslongchamp, and his exclusive release and signing of his writing endeavor, voted Best Read in *Westword's* Best of Denver. It is featured on the front page of *Out Front Magazine* and the elusive pick for Oprah's Book of the Month - "Amplify – My Oh My.

"Kent, you must be feeling fine with all this elation. Is this the defining moment of your heart's desire?"

"Well Duh Dan, look around you? This is a magnificent moment for me! For over 30 years, I have worked on this project. I have given up so many times and really thought this day would never come! But, right here, right now, this extraordinary moment is here, it is all unfolding right before my eyes, and what an amazing sight to see!"

"Kent, I must ask, why over 30 years to get to this moment? What kept you from achieving this goal and reaching your heart's desire long before this day?"

"Dan, to be honest, only one thing kept me from this moment, it was ME, MYSELF, and I. I filled my heart and soul with self-doubt and low self-esteem. I became my own worst enemy. I drenched myself in negativity and drained myself of anything positive. I lived year to year in desolation and darkness. Then, the workshop happened, and in this unexpected magical moment, my life was changed. I was transformed, and this is what life has become for me. I still must pinch myself at times to believe this is all real and happening to me!"

"So, with everything happening so fast, have you really put the past behind you? Or do you really think this is it? Is this a defining moment in your life or is this the last dance, the magic gone, the party over, the darkness and desolation set in, and just like a candle in the wind, your light is extinguished?"

"Oh Dan, Dan. Desperate Dan, I know that is what you want to hear, the big story, no more glory! But let me tell you what, Dan. The botched Botox protruding from your bloated lips must have breached your brain… It took me 30 years to push past my own binding bondage of beliefs, and in one defining moment, 16 hours, the whole extent of this writing workshop, those bonds vanished. The bonds that tied me down for so long were cut free. Dan, I broke away from the belly of the beast and all its burdens. If you think for one second that I will allow that to happen to me again, just like Taylor Swift, I am telling you that I will never, ever, ever, ever, for any reason, under any circumstances, allow for that to happen again, like ever."

"Oh Kent, how can you say that you will never ever allow that? Never ever is a long time, like forever! And because your amplified voice is limited to a group of 5 letters LGBTQ, I cannot help but wonder if your peak is past?"

"Oh, my Dipstick Dan, I see you, and oh my, I would not want to be you! Let me ask you a question. Do you see this petty act of desperation as your defining moment of defeat or is this just another defining moment, like so many that you have had, that demonstrates your pure stupidity? What, speechless? That's probably a good thing. But that look on your face says it all. And so does the sweat, running down your forehead and melting your makeup, unmasking your—good lord, so many wrinkles, popping out like pimples on a pre-teen.

"FYI, had you done your research Dan, you might have discovered some interesting facts and information about those five letters LGBTQ. How many letters are in the alphabet? Twenty-six Dan. Even if you used your toes and fingers, the number is too big, so I helped you out a little. You made the blatantly wrong statement that the LGBTQ+ community is limited. Much like your ego and the wig you're wearing to cover your receding hairline, but DoucheBag Dan. The 16 letters that define our ever growing, diversified, and endlessly expanding community's acronym of orientations is now, LGBTIQCAPGNGFNBA that stands for Lesbian, Gay, Bisexual, Transgender Intersex, Queer/Questioning, Curious, Asexual, Pansexual, Gender-Nonconforming, Gender-Fluid, Non-Binary, and Androgynous. Add to those the other thirty-six sexual identities, and that brings the rather extensive and expanding letters representing our community to a grand total of 52 Dan. So, let me ask you this, do you think that your career is limited by the acronym of 7 letters that defines you best, ASSHOLE!?"

"Just who do you think you are that you can talk to me, Dan D Denver, that way?"

"Oh, Duped Dan, I know who I am. And maybe you better get that short-term memory looked at. At your age, it could be the beginning of senility. I am the legendary and limitless Kent Deslongchamp, a name that will never be forgotten, especially after this interview hits the sordid cyber circles. So, Ta Ta for now Dan, gotta run. I have this little event that I need to get to because, in case you forgot, I am the guest of honor. Nice to see you Mimosa, ravishing as always, *kiss kiss*. And Thropple, you left your jock over at the house, again. Can I expect you later to pick it up? Thanks, Dorky Dan for the buzz, banter, and branding. Ah the night is young, and oooohhhh, so is that hottie over there in line to get—hmmm, oh yes, my signature <*evil grin*> and possibly something to write my next book about. Did I say that out loud? Oh, yes, I did indeed, amplified, and proud. Just one more thing before I go and meet that young stray, then I am on my way. Ain't it just fabulous to live life so Gay!? Happy Gay Way, that's all I've got to say."

This writing piece is based upon these 3 reasons Why I Write and resonates with my personal values and convictions. To INSPIRE those who can't, won't, don't or are incapable, to speak out, be out, or stand out. To BELIEVE in yourself, live as yourself and to love yourself, with all your heart, all your soul and all you might, every day. To CONNECT with those oppressed, those unsure and those in need, and all who are a letter in the LGBTIQCAPGNGFNBA community and beyond.

What is Your Writing Goal? Reason 1 - Inspiring Others, Reason 2 - Fulfilling a Passion, Reason - 3 Connecting with Readers

SELF-REFLECTIVE SUPERHERO

I don't know if, because my name is Kent, and that Kent is part of the name of Clark Kent (AKA Superman), that a cosmic connection was created or a superfluous interface with the factors that collaborate Who I am, What I am, How I am or Why I am. The relationship of Clark Kent to his alter identity Superman. Clark Kent, is the clever facade of the ordinary, hiding the extraordinary, the mundane masquerading as the Super Human, the mild mannered cloaking the superpowers, and the display of vulnerabilities concealing the true hero within. Clark Kent, chooses the outward illusions, exemplifying his weaknesses, his cowardliness, his disabilities, and instills the personas and stereotypes of being spineless, inadequate, and weak. All of these traits conceal the true characteristics, true empowerment and true identity the Super Hero, the Super Human, and the Super Man, he truly is.

Much like Clark Kent, I hid behind a facade on the outside with the true hero kept secret within. I displayed the expected normalized ordinary appearance of a young, white, Catholic, American boy; crew cut hair, jeans, tennis shoes and on Sunday switching out to a pressed, clean suit and tie. Upheld the mundane, wearing nothing colorful, stoic gestures displaying no animated or feminine body movements. I chose to exemplify my vulnerabilities with manly mannerisms, no show of emotion, displaying obedience and expressing interest in sports, cars, and physical activities. I chose the persona of being introverted, uncompassionate, and lastly, although i wore no glasses, a symbolic optical aid impaired my true vision and blocked off the true me within, all to create the expected normal identity on the outside, and defer, the disillusion of the identity inside.

This dual relationship within myself was maintained and flowed seamlessly, with no visible conflict for many years, as did Clark Kent's with his alter self, Superman. It was not until Clark Kent began to wrestle with his secrets, the betrayal to himself, the fear of discovery, the cost of hiding and the emotional battles which stemmed from this duality, that conflict arose and was a force to reckon with. Like Clark Kent, I echoed the same conflicts, wrestling with my secrets, betrayal to myself, my family, fear of discovery, the emotional costs to hiding and the toll of this constant, daily growing, struggle for dual identity.

When the role of Superman the Superhero was needed to manifest, to move forward, take control and come alive, the change began with the removal of Clark Kent's identity, his glasses. This signifies that Clark Kent is no longer present, that Superman no longer needs to hide, the transformation continues, with the business attire shed, as is any essence of Clark Kent. Now, unfurled stands a Super Hero, a Super Man. The attire, a bright red cape, boots, and speedo-style outer briefs, skintight blue leotard and a tight long-sleeved blue shirt, showing the chiseled and muscular physique. The outfit is accented with a bright yellow belt and dawning in the middle of his chest a large red 'S' on a yellow diamond-shaped shield with red borders, the renowned emblem and identity of Superman the embodiment of hope, peace, justice, truth, and identity. In the end Clark Kent and Superman learn to embrace their duality and honor the cosmic creed to see and be seen. Unity is achieved and conflict resolved.

The discovery of self, self-expression, self-image, self-esteem, self-identity, and sexuality laid the groundwork for the numerous conflicts I manifested or stemmed from the causes and effects of others. Books became my escape, my fantasy to live vicariously, to cloak the harsh realities of life, to save worlds when I couldn't even save myself, to live as anything other than me, to be a hero when I felt I was a failure, to be proud, out, filled with unbridled spirit, to display flamboyance in flaming flare unapologetically. My journals, my writings, my stories that I filled page after page with, gave me the means to enter on that blank page a unique, personal tool to conquer and defeat whatever was needed for that moment, that emotion, that struggle. This monumental discovery, that like books, writing was another creation of my own means, my own ways, in my own unique style, and my own words, solely created for me alone to let go, let be and let live; my created place where I never suffered the consequences in living my life; never dealt with the detriments for expressing my femininity or endured the hate and animosity for embracing my uniqueness, and never reached the extreme emotional breakdowns of depression, solitude, self-hate, and self-harm.

I quickly learned writing was a gift that served my purpose and a means to communicate with others. I discovered that others would endure my expressions, my beliefs, hear my desires, and consider my views. It was a shock to be heard without interruption, without immediate judgment, to not be overshadowed by others' interjections; to be able to say what was on my mind. I discovered that I was able to procure more positive outcomes, incur less negativity, my actions less compromising, and promising outcomes without emotional detriments. Writing also gave the recipient the same opportunities to get the same results and procure the same outcomes in the same light, in the same way, with the same means.

My whole life, I have embellished my world, with words which aid me to untangle my thoughts, invent my ideas, divulge in my desires, visualize my views, dazzle my dreams, harbor my hopes, dissolve my defeats, and doodle away despair. I have written journals, stories, poems, mantras and even in the use of a single solitary significant word. In reading a book or writing a book, it is my belief that anything, everything, and all things can be, and there is not one thing, zero, absolutely nothing that can ever become. The impossible is always possible, and the unimaginable can always become reality.

This is why I write, this is why I create the stories of my life. This is why I am what I am, unlike the black ink that forms letters on the white pages they are penned upon. Writing allows me, Kent, to explore without limitations everything about me, every aspect of me, every dream, hope, desire, and thought that I alone can construct. I know that even with nothing, something can be found. From that something the embodiment of vision and purpose can always be found. This found purpose is given a voice through words. The words are then presented in harmonious synchronicity, conducted with my melodic expression, the symphony of syllables, segue the paragraphs into sonatas leading the story into a crescendo of the collective written work, building and climaxing with resonance, reason relevance the mesmerizing moment memorializing each of you in your authorship and soul mastermind of your melded masterpiece for all to enjoy.

I thrive on this attention, setting me center stage in the spotlight, standing in full view, for all to see. No barrier, no borders, no boundaries, no binds, putting everything out there. Giving my all, without holding back, without restriction, living in that moment to the fullest potential, without regret, expecting nothing in return, unconditionally giving my heart, my mind, my body and my soul. This is the ultimate moment for me to be fully present, taking in every detail, every aspect, immersed in just being Who I am, What I am, How I am. This workshop was this moment, this feeling over and over, again and again. Thank You. In appreciation for the journey to "Finding My Voice" and much gratitude for the outcome of this journey "Amplifying My Voice".

ABOUT AUTHOR KENT DESLONGCHAMP

I was born under the crescent moon, of a star filled winter Colorado sky at 11:36 pm, at Rose Medical Center in Denver, Colorado on December 1, 1961. From my first breath, the fierceness of the Fire sign Sagittarius blazed into my soul, the desire to seek out adventures activated, and the presence of my powerful, plentiful personality and passionate persona permeated into every crevice in my delivery room. Today, these beliefs still permeate every crevice of my life, however they are emulated, empowered, and enhanced by 62 years, still personified in everyone I meet, everywhere I go, every moment I experience, and in everything that I do. They require no effort, they are natural, synchronized aspects that are part of my being, like my breathing is to life.

These core principles are the constants that enrich my life and bring the joys, delights, happinesses, and the loves that I experience as a Sagittarius, human being, and Kent Deslongchamp. These moments have given means to and instilled in my whole self, my cores in reasoning, my cores upon which my life foundations are built, and the cores my pillars of beliefs are lived by. These powers, convictions, presences, passions, and fierceness are my essential essences that roll over into my writing.

From elementary school, all the way through high school, and even college, I had the pleasure and presence of writing, in many forms, as a part of my life. Me, being on the newspaper in elementary, junior, and senior high school taught the basic questions to ask when writing: who, what, when, where, why, and how. For self-expression, personal vision, and daily diversions, I used journal writing, free flow and short stories. When in conflict, in defense or cause of a dilemma, I wrote detailed and descriptive personal letters to allow for my viewpoint to be expressed without interruption, and feedback could be returned without interference; open communication could be achieved. I have taken every kind of class, every kind of course, every kind of session, every kind of lab one can take for writing from the mechanics of writing, the styles of writing and genres of writing. I have written projects from self-help, educational curriculum, non-fiction, historical, and autobiographical.

It was not until this workshop that I pursued, invested in, or made the time for and completed all aspects, means or ways of publishing my many written works. This workshop has given me the basics to pursue, enrich and compose my own personal journeys, my personal vast writing projects, and each of the steps along the way to accomplish this. The producing, printing, publishing and marketing aspects, along with the vast knowledge bases learned, in the numerous platforms, editing cost, formatting choices, financial aspects, creative expressions, personal values, complete the whole journey in finding my voice, writing my voice, capturing my voice, editing my voice, quality assurance of my voice, validation of my voice, amplifying my voice, marketing strategies for my voice, and concluding with publishing, printing and continued monitoring from sales and revenue from my voice. This now gives me the collective and learned opportunity to bring about anything and everything of the vast writing realms from beginning to the end of the authorship dream. *The Nudge to Write* is my fist published written work and with this under my belt, this bucket list check mark completed, I can only imagine what the future will unfold, the magnificent purpose-driven visions ahead, dreams, opportunities, and moments that will be ventured into and the ecclesiastical and soul enriched places each will take me to. To all of you, the readers, my muses, and soulful followers, you get front row tickets to this unique and one of kind experience, energy exchange, mindful and enriching authorship experience with me, the one and only, Kent Deslongchamp. I look forward to and cherish each step on this road. With thankfulness and gratitude.

PASSION STATEMENT

I write with an unwavering passion in the genre of Creative Nonfiction. I favor it because it reflects and suits my personality and makes possible the ability to convey, through words, a vivid and distinct picture of me and who I am in my own fanciful flair. This genre also gives me the fuel which burns my conviction to believe in not only in who I am, but also what I am, what I have to say, and how I want to say it. This has been, and always will be, my personal belief system and core within myself. Self-expression, self-freedom, and self-development are powerful means of alleviating self-doubt, self-denial, self-destruction or self-defeat. One of my earliest childhood memories comes from my elementary school days. I meticulously wrote in my Indian tablet with my sharpened #2 pencil, watching as others chatted between themselves or sat in defiance, doing nothing. For me, it was a catalyst that empowered me to discover my self-beauty and self-love; to break free from my parents, dissolving their values and expectations, invalidating their perspectives of how they envisioned me and what they thought best for me; what they expected me to become, their impermissible restrictions allowing for no room, no compromise, no understanding, nor give room to grow, or to build self-acceptance, instill self-apprecia-tions, or express my delights found in the opportunities and discoveries within the many facets of life that I ventured down. The hearing of whispers from the universe in offering direction along the uncharted roads and pathways, guiding me through life's labyrinth and leading me away from their boundaries, unlocking the binds placed upon me, opening the doorways to endless possibilities and the pursuit of the unimaginable. Without this pursuit of the unimaginable, I would have remained a mere echo of my ordinary existence, never venturing out to discover the odyssey of my true voice, my true gift which I penned in my writing, strengthened with my foundation and anchored in the core belief that by living life with benevolent concern, your life will lead you in the directions to pursue your passions. Your passions lead you in finding your purpose. When your pursue your pur-pose with the highest conviction and set your intention to reach for your wildest dream that anything and everything is possible and that you alone are the sole author to deter-mine what lies ahead in your procurement of unlimited realms of possibility and finding your infinity and beyond.

MY NUDGE TO WRITE: IN THE BEGINNING...
BY TONYA ROCHE

I hear the whispers of stories in my mind. They have always been there. Like imaginary friends.

In the beginning, as a child, these stories came out in the way of play-acting. My closest cousin and I would pretend to be famous singers, standing on our makeshift stage made of sawed logs, stacked and waiting for the wood stove, and belting out the lyrics of *Delta Dawn*—as though we could actually carry a tune.

We would have elaborate backstories. Our world, built only within our vivid imaginations, looked nothing like our reality. But we could see it clearly. We lived it during those moments of play and we described our setting in a way that could draw any other cousin or sibling (willing to play along) into it. These stories could go on for days at a time during the summer breaks from school, coming out of our concocted realm only when forced by parents who just didn't understand our dedication to this marvelous, made-up milieu.

I never questioned "how" these stories came to me. They were always just an accepted part of myself.

As soon as I could read, I devoured as many books as I could. The school library was my favorite hangout. I would even volunteer to work there whenever I had free time. I think at one point, I imagined I would grow up to be a librarian, and be surrounded by books every day—forever.

Stories and books brought me joy. They pulled me into worlds that I hadn't yet imagined. They hooked me, heart and soul. Through them, I traveled back in time, and caught glimpses of possible futures. I thought, one day, my stories would bring this kind of joy to others.

I started writing as soon as I understood the concept of self-expression on paper. I journaled… a lot. What began as getting my frustrations out on paper eventually led to more positive thoughts and short stories for my own entertainment.

I wrote dozens of poems, many dark, but some uplifting and happy. I submitted a few to local periodicals that hosted small writing contests. I even won one. It was a proud moment.

But, as happens to most of us, reality ultimately closed in. Real life took priority over my imaginary life, and eventually, that fictitious world slipped away. In its place were logic, responsibility, and the determination to just survive. The necessity to be an adult subdued, and finally, silenced my inner child. There was no room for her in my life now, so she obediently drifted to a dark, secluded corner of my mind to sit quietly, knowing she was destined to fade into nothingness. Sad and forgotten.

A SPARK…

The birth of a child is life-changing, sparking feelings that, even though expected, still shocks us when it hits. Protectiveness. Such intense love. Pride. Anxiety (what if I can't take care of this new little human?). Possessiveness. Socially, this is considered an "adult" responsibility, requiring mature, grown-up actions and decisions. A child cannot raise a child, right?

But this is when my own inner-child lit a tiny spark, reminding me she was still there, waiting to report for duty. She was faint. Weak, but determined to see the light. You see, one cannot raise a child on logic alone. Strict rules. All work and no play. These are the tools for failed parenthood. One needs the help of one's imagination. Their inner-child.

I no longer lived in my fictional worlds from childhood, but I could once more dip my toes in those imaginary waters of my stories, showing my children the wonderful magic of make-believe.

I encouraged "pretending", but not lying. I was absolute in showing them the difference. They wrote plays and acted them out for me. I was their adoring audience.

We made up stories and games together. When times were tough, we used our imaginations to write ourselves into scripts to entertain us when weather prevented outdoor fun. We took ourselves out for dinner and a movie, right there in our own living room. We built forts, and fought monsters and crocodiles.

My inner-child was vibrant and active once more. I bought beautiful notebooks in the hopes that they would inspire me to start writing again, but the occasional journal entry was all I could ever manage. It was ok, though, because my stories lived through my children, and that was enough for now. My time to write would come one day.

As the children grew older, their need for imaginary entertainment was replaced with sports, school work, friends, and reality. They simply outgrew our pretend universes. I still called upon my inner-child when I needed creative ways to communicate with my teenagers as I was now perceived as an enemy of their free will. She was very proficient in her new responsibility. To this day, my kids reminisce about my creative parenting techniques. They even use a few of them with my grandchildren.

THE IGNITION...

What has all of this to do with my writing journey? Imagination. Creativity. Stories. Releasing that inner-child. One needs to let go of the seriousness long enough to allow the creativity to flow.

My life was so chaotic during this time. I was wound so tightly, the logical side of my brain overshadowed my creative side. My compositions were limited to technical writings: standard operating procedures, maintenance manuals, requirements, proposals. I could feel my inner-child cowering from the horror of it all. But those sterile, unimaginative words on paper paid the bills.

This chaos often disrupted my schedule and left my family sitting on the back-burner. One day, the frenzy caused me to be late getting home. My son had soccer practice that night so it was a mad dash to get him out the door and on our way to the playing fields.

It was a beautiful autumn afternoon—my favorite time of year. The leaves were just starting to change color and the air was filled with the sweet cologne of humus. Summer's warmth faded into early autumn crispness. My son and I made a game of identifying trees along the way. Bright yellow leaves clung to the sugar maples. Thick trunks with sprawling fat limbs of the mighty oak dotted the fields and thickets. I let my attention stray from the road just a second too long, and the car swerved. It was just enough to bring my attention back to the wheel where it should have been all along.

"Mom!" chided my son. "Pay attention to the road."

So sensible, even at the young age of 11.

Then, the unthinkable happened. We were startled by a loud "pop" coming from the rear passenger side of the car, and the steering wheel jerked in my hands. I gripped tighter as the car was pulled toward a steep bank on the right. The car took on a life of its own. In an attempt to pull the car back onto the road, I over-compensated and we careened across oncoming traffic and onto the embankment on the opposite side of the road.

Leaves and debris showered over the hood and windshield of the car. We finally came to rest, precariously on the bank, our bodies lurching forward from the sudden stop. Before I could breathe a sigh of relief, the car started to tilt as though it were going to roll but something prevented us from tipping too far. All four tires settled back onto the ground.

Neither of us could say a word. I looked at my son; he was pale and shaking.

"Are you ok?" I asked.

He nodded, but didn't speak. After several deep breaths and inaudible obscenities to calm my nerves, I inched the Honda forward, off the embankment and back onto the road. The sound of metal on macadam confirmed our tire had blown. As I pulled my spare tire out, I uttered a silent prayer of gratitude. This wasn't as bad as it could have been.

That night, after we were back home and safe, I couldn't let go of what had happened. What "could" have happened. My imagination ran wild, and not in a good way. I started going over "what ifs".

What if I hadn't been able to pull the car from the steep drop off after the tire had blown?

What if there had been more traffic on the road?

What if the car had not stopped tilting?

What if we had actually rolled? My son could have been seriously injured, or even killed.

A macabre story began to unfold in my mind. I filled notebooks with my "what ifs". They haunted me for many years. Many times I tried to write the story that was banging around in my brain. My inner-child wanted nothing to do with this one. She cowered in the shadows of my mind. I eventually forgot she existed. I was on my own with this story.

THE HAUNTING...

The accident brought about nightmares for years. I became more protective and obsessive with my children. I saw the accident in my dreams, but in them, it ended very differently. Many mornings I would wake up with tears in my eyes. I knew how this horror story in my mind ended. I knew the only way to make the nightmares stop was to get the story down on paper. So that's what I did.

There were many brain-dumps, outlines, and short scenes jotted down in half-a-dozen notebooks. I still didn't have the mental drive to focus on any long-form writing. Life was chaotic. But the story was always there. For more than 15 years, it haunted me.

I created blog spaces to release my pent up writing urges. I blogged about workplace politics, riddled with humor and satire. I wrote witty magazine articles on fashion trends. I turned my attention toward safe topics and media, steering clear of the dark tale with which my mind was obsessed.

But it would not be forgotten. The story wanted to be told. Needed to be heard. And so, I relented. I wrote the beginning. I wrote a bit of the middle. And I wrote an ending. And that was enough. The hauntings stopped. It wouldn't be forgotten, but it would no longer plague my dreams.

The story sat there like that, less than half finished until I retired from my demanding engineering career.

PAST MY PRIME...

You would think the story stopped there. I have all the time in the world to write now. What could possibly hold me back?

Me. I held myself back. I was so accustomed to the adrenaline high of the demanding job, I didn't know how to slow down and let my creativity flow. I had become so tightly-wound, so serious, so logical, I convinced myself I needed to be doing something useful. Writing was fine to fill in the gaps between practical activities, but it waned in priority as I piled more and more outside activities into my schedule.

I got involved in volunteer work. Non-profits were great organizations where I could put my lifetime skills to use. I took on more and more, until I realized I was chasing that same adrenaline high that I had become addicted to during my 35 years of working in high-profile positions. It was that same addiction that wore me down and took over my life for so long. Writing once again took a back seat.

At this rate, I would never get my story written. Time was not on my side. I was convinced I was too old to ever become a writer of any merit. And that inner-child? I had forgotten she ever existed. When did I stop having fun? When did I lose my glimmer, my joy? Did I have any spark left in me? Writing still had a hold on my heart. If I was going to follow my dreams of becoming a published author, something needed to change.

A local writing group started at the library in my rural county. These sorts of events were rare. Here was an opportunity to hang out with like-minded people. Creatives. Writers. It was the motivation I needed. I would soon learn that everyone else in our small group was half my age or younger. Rather than see this as a negative, I embraced the experience and had a blast!

There were fun little writing prompts. I let my silliness rule my writing in these groups and gradually coaxed my inner-child out of hibernation. She was stiff and clumsy at first, but the enthusiasm of our fellow writers soon brought her out of her shell. She was once again hard at work. We were loving our stories, again.

This group is where I first heard about an annual event called NaNoWriMo (National Novel Writing Month). In November, NaNoWriMo hosts a writing challenge to write 50,000 words of a novel in 30 days. Sounds easy, right? I had to give it a shot.

It was brutal! Exhausting! I never knew writing could take so much energy. This first writing event is when Inner-child and I met Muse.

MEET THE MUSE...

I liken my muse to a skittish little sprite. The first time I met her, I didn't recognize her. She was bashful and quiet. Tentative. Not very vocal at all. She felt like an annoying buzzing in my mind; another manifestation of a guilty conscience when I sat down and tried to write.

Inner-child was not helpful in pinpointing this vexing phenomenon. She would dance around Muse, cloaking her identity and courting my attention like a petulant spoiled youth.

Muse was (and continues to be) easily scared off, chased away by my irritations and frustrations. She would quickly disappear at the first sign of a distraction, of anything that pulled my attention from writing.

As she got braver, her intentions became more clear to me. I understood her purpose. I listened, and together, our stories finally started to come alive.

Muse is less timid now. Her irritations with me are louder and clearer than ever. She is a tiny bit selfish, demanding my undivided concentration. She cannot, or will not, share my attention with anything or anyone else. The first sign of my mind wandering, she warns me by pulling the story away, hiding it behind a billowy veil. She refuses to return it until I have blocked all other distractions, and she once again has my undivided attention.

If I do not immediately heed her warning, she obstinately crosses her arms, stomps her tiny sprite foot, and flits away in a cloud of pixie dust (or sprite dust), taking her inspiration with her.

Muse, Inner-child and I have learned to work well together these days. We are most productive when we are dancing about gracefully in unison in our fictional worlds. Our performances are like a choreographed ballet, the soft orchestral music whispering in the background. Feet float on air. Arms lifted, swaying in synchronicity.

Some days, the words come gushing out, hot and furious. I type quickly, lest a syllable or a sentence gets away from me. The narrator in my mind dictates faster than I can type or write. Days like these are both exhilarating and exhausting. The excitement is in documenting the words. When the mental recitation stops, and there is nothing left to write, I feel empty and drained, in need of refilling the creative well; or I need rest.

THE CHALLENGE....

That first NaNoWriMo, I did not "win". I did not write 50,000 words. I did not pass GO. I did not collect $200. Well, there is no monetary reward for NaNo, but I didn't meet my goal of writing 50,000 words. I did, however, write 25,000 words, which was 25,000 more than I had ever officially written before. So I called it a win. I was hooked.

I have participated in a few National Novel Writing Months over the years. I have "won" a few, and I have fallen short a few times, but I have never considered any of the challenges to be failures. They have offered me the motivation, focus, and sense of community I needed to get the creative juices flowing. I learned to set goals, and have fun chasing them.

The handful of lessons I have learned during this writing journey is that I always need to keep things exciting. Interesting. Fun. Fresh. When the act of writing stops being fun or exciting, the progression of writing simply stops altogether. I realize I need to find creative ways to stay motivated.

If you find you've lost that spark that normally brings you so much joy, don't be afraid of creative motivation methods. Nothing is too eccentric or woo-woo. Find your muse. Release your inner-child. Figure out what inspires you. What gets you excited to jump out of bed in the morning?

If you need to set intentions or manifest a writing career, set those intentions. If you are a planner and do better setting realistic goals, then plan out your writing path. If vision boards get your juices flowing, break out the cardboard and magazines and get your vision glued down. Let your spirits be your guide. Short of breaking the law, any means of motivation is fair game. Get creative!

Discover *your* magical journey.

NOW, ABOUT THAT ELEPHANT IN THE ROOM...

I hear you. Your voice is faint and distant, but I know you're there. Yours is the voice for which I listen in my time of need. You are a comfort to me. Your words are those of encouragement.

I hear you, but I do not see your face. I do not know who you are, or where you are. You are not near, but I know that you are coming.

These days, I am lost. Unseen. I am desperate to find my purpose in life, but it eludes me. I slog through days, weeks, even months looking for answers that will not come. I occupy my idle time with unfulfilling activities. I find little pleasure in them.

My days sap my energy. I tire quickly. My motivation is low. At night, though, I toss and turn, dreaming of things I cannot accomplish. Haunted by memories I cannot change. Longing for the confidence I once possessed.

I tell myself I am a writer. I am enough. But I shun my affirmations and sabotage my progress. Then, you reach out to me, and I am comforted. My mind calms, and I write for a while, enjoying the tranquility of unhindered creativity.

There was once a time when I was blessed with self-confidence, motivation and energy. Those were my "important" years. My "useful" years. My "successful" years. I had a clear purpose then. I thrived in my society's defined values system.

I often found myself pondering my dilemma. I had been looking forward to retirement, but what does one do when one has aged out of her society's values? I no longer have a successful career. My children are grown and no longer need me. My contributions to the household finances are minuscule. What is my worth, then? All those things that previously defined success were behind me. I needed to redefine my own system of values.

What better way to pull myself from the depths of self-pity than a trip to the coffee shop and a bout of retail therapy. The weight on my shoulders lighten in anticipation of the day of exploration ahead. Today, something magical could happen.

It is a gorgeous spring day in Texas. My daughter and I decide to explore a town near her home that I have never been to before, being only a semi-annual visitor there. It is small enough that we can park the car, and walk all over the cozy borough.

There are so many fun, unique shops; antique shops, clothing stores, thrift shops, restaurants and coffee shops. Retail heaven.

I am waiting for you.

The voice in my head is soothing. I should question my sanity, but I don't. I just listen. Draw it in like a breath. It lingers there, warming my heart.

A whiff of espresso and steamed milk pulls me from my thoughts; my daughter and I follow the scent to a charming little cafe on the corner. Is there a more invigorating aroma than that of rich, earthy coffee? Perhaps the bitter flavor of espresso smoothed by the silkiness of milk would be a worthy contender against my racing mind.

Taking in the scenery, my writer's mind summons pages of mental commentary—of prose and verse. The smooth mahogany tables line walls of cozy prints in warm, soothing tones. Dim lights cast a buttery soft glow throughout the cafe. The soft din of voices merge together in easy harmony, a tune that could only exist in a coffee shop.

Easing itself through the low buzz of human expression, the voice is in my ear again.

Soon. So near. I am here.

Back in the afternoon sunshine, I automatically turn toward an inconspicuous shop tucked in the shadow of a large newer clothing shop. We pass display windows filled with brightly colored, quilted bags slung across mannequins' shoulders. Flowy summer dresses in every hue. My daughter comments that this is definitely a store for me, but I walk past it, drawn to the tiny shop behind it.

A spark of prickling energy hits me, raising goosebumps on my arms. There is magic here. We enter the surprisingly sizable solitary room, the coolness a contrast to the heat of the outdoors. The space is filled with glass displays containing large bowls of every crystal and stone imaginable. Lighted cases with mirrors dot the middle of the boutique. In them are statues—hearts, mushrooms and other shapes crafted from smooth stones of many color combinations.

I pick up a small pink heart and hold it in my palm. A little green toadstool sits in the middle of the next case. These two shall come home with me. The little space makes me smile. I could spend hours in here, it's so calming.

Joining another gathering of patrons, we examine a case full of carved stone animals. Tiny frogs. Wolves. Dragonflies. I see him, then. The magic that called to me.

A beautiful desert jasper elephant stands proudly in the center of the lighted case. His image is reflected on four sides by mirrors, the fifth side, the front, open for view. The world around me disappears as I draw near the case, eyes focused only on the statue.

Reaching into the case, I gingerly draw it out, feeling its energy. I just have to take this charming little pachyderm home with me.

Cupping it in my hands, I hold it to my chest and whisper, "You are the one. I found you."

In answer, the stone statue releases his grounding energy. His comforting glow spreads through me, warming my body and calming my mind, forever binding our spirits.

THE END, OR JUST THE BEGINNING?

Every day is a new beginning. The jasper elephant and I have begun a new journey of creative discovery together. The elephant, Muse, the inner-child, and I…the four of us, all working together. Sounds childish, right?

With each passing day, I feel the weight of adulthood slowly lifting from my shoulders. Through writing, I have rediscovered the joy of play and the boundless possibilities of imagination. And though life will never be without its challenges, I know that as long as I have my pen in hand, my notebooks, and my laptop, I will always find my way back to the world of make-believe.

ABOUT AUTHOR TONYA ROCHE

 I enjoy writing stories that end with unexpected twists. I lose myself in fictitious worlds, filling them with adventure and surprises. In presenting unlikely scenarios, I aspire to compel readers to believe anything is possible, and find themselves feeling as though they are part of the experience.

I strive to provoke the readers' hopes and dreams, play on their fears. Take them on a roller coaster ride of emotions. Stories are our portals to escape the mundane world into magical realms where we become sleuths and heroes. We fight demons and monsters. Slay dragons. Fall in love. As an author, my goal is to pull readers into the tale and hold them hostage without realizing they've been captured.

I write to bring joy to myself and to others. To entertain. To spark imagination. Through my work, I hope to give back a thread of joy that I have always found through my own experience with reading.

My own love of literature goes back to childhood. From fairytales to biographies, I read them all, devouring books as though they might disappear before I could read them all. I laughed. I cried. I cowered on the kitchen floor while reading a paperback about vampires. My favorite books were those that moved me through a range of emotions, and left me thinking about them long after the book had been returned to the library.

At the heart of my work, what I value most are things such as adventure and curiosity, highlighting fun and imagination. The presentation of a pleasurable experience. I aim for creative uniqueness with a hearty side of humor, whenever possible. I believe literature has the power to challenge our perspectives and learned beliefs, opening our minds to the possibility of an alternative reality.

My writing is an extension of myself. A look inside the workings of a creative mind. The ego of a story-teller. A way for me to reach out and connect with others who share my desire for adventure. Thank you for joining me in my world of pure fantasy and the occasional magical encounter.

If you like, please follow me on REAM.
https://reamstories.com/lqn28jbnud

Warm regards,
Tonya Roche

Writing
PROMPTS

NOSTALGIC BITES
WRITING PROMPT

Before starting our writing and self-publishing workshops, we encourage writers to join our community board on Heylo (https://heylo.group/write-and-publish). This is a supportive way for writers and community supporters, like yourself, to keep in touch with each other. For the folks participating in this round of workshops, we wanted to have them introduce themselves to each other by using the universal language of food.

NOSTALGIC BITES PROMPT:

Begin your writing journey by introducing yourself and delving into the realm of your most cherished childhood memories—specifically, the delectable dish that holds a special place in your heart. Transport your readers to the essence of your past by vividly describing this favorite dish using the five senses.

This prompt was a fun and insightful way to get to know each other outside of the typical sharing of names and locations. It also challenged the writers to practice world-building (often used in fictional books but, in this case, applied to a real-life memory in the past) to use words to teleport readers back to a place through the five senses: touch, taste, smell, sight, and hearing.

We invite you to join our community on Heylo (https://heylo.group/write-and-publish). Introduce yourself and connect with others.

HAM POT PIE - THE PENNSYLVANIA DUTCH WAY

I was born and raised in the hills of Pennsylvania, a cultural mash-up of Pennsylvania Dutch and Appalachia. "Cookery" played an important role in our family. Meals weren't simply nourishment, although that was important, too. Meals were magical potions filled with warmth and love. A sense of security and safety comes to mind when I think about my favorite Pennsylvania Dutch meal. Ham Pot-pie (or bott boi as it was originally called).

Contrary to how it sounds, pot-pie is not a pie made with pie crust. There is no gravy in this hearty dish. The dish is brothy and full of flavor, with chewy homemade noodles that add the perfect texture to the dish.

My mother and grandmother would work together, mixing dough in giant ceramic bowls, using only a recipe that they had memorized. No recipe cards or cookbooks were pulled out for these occasions. Using well-loved rolling pins handed down through generations, they would flatten the dough out on the kitchen table. This flour mixture was slightly thicker than typical Italian pasta. Mom and grandma sliced the dough into wide noodles, let them dry for a minute, and boiled them in a pot of ham broth until they were tender.

This was my ultimate comfort food growing up. Salty and savory. Substantial, chewy noodles that absorbed the taste of the briny broth in which they were cooked. The perfect Sunday dinner.

The entire house would be warmed with the scent of cured meat. The smell made my mouth water and my tummy rumble with desire. It was all I could do to not pluck a juicy chunk of ham from the pot before the whole meal was set on the table.

The entire family would sit around several tables set up for large gatherings. Grandparents. Parents. Children and grandchildren. Cousins, aunts and uncles. The pot pie was served piping hot in generous bowls, with fresh chopped raw onion sprinkled on top. The crunchiness of the raw onion perfectly balances the chewiness of the warm noodles.

Warm homemade bread with homemade apple butter were the only accompaniments we needed with this meal, but salads were usually part of the spread, as well. Sweet fruit salads as well as lettuce and onion salad with a home-made creamy dressing. Home-canned mustard pickles, tart and sharp, rounded out the hearty dinner.

Is your mouth watering, yet? Mine is.

~TONYA ROCHE

KENT'S COLLECTIVE CRAZY COLORFUL CHRISTMAS COOKIE AND CANDY CELEBRATION AND COLLABORATION STORY

~~~~~~~~~~~~~~~~~~~~~~~~~~~~~~~~~~~~~~

Breathing to me is not just a function of the human body, a mechanical response from the muscles in the lungs, the inhale of oxygen and the exhale of carbon dioxide. It is so much more. It is a daily mindset, a envisionary tool I use for my well-being at the start and end to each day. It is a pattern, a practice, a flow, a methodical, melodious routine, an air affirmation, an appreciation for all, a meditative motion, a mindful mantra, and the breath of life, enriching each morning, bringing balance, building fortitude upon the foundation from which my life is built. It is my beginning, the Ying (inhale), and my ending, the Yang (exhale). The acknowledgment and acclamation at the end of the day of thankfulness and in gratitude, slowing the breaths in mesmerizing melding breaths, until sleep envelopes the body, mind and soul. Then again in the morning, beginning again, breathing in and out. It is in this simple practice that I prepare myself, for this moment in time.

Ah! I take a deep breath. The smell from the newly opened ream of paper fills my nostrils. I hold the oxygen in my lungs, simultaneously, my eyes take in the essence of the quiet dimly lit room, then slowly release the air back out. Again, breathe in, this time close my eyes, heighten my other senses, hold the air in, feel the chest muscles relaxing, release the tension, my body rejuvenated, and my mind refreshed, then take in one more deep, four-second long, engaged, focused breath, saying silently to myself "take in the best" each breath in, and then release the carbon dioxide back to the universe silently saying, "let go of the rest". I pause, allow the moment, the solitude, the calmness, and the cool air to envelope my body, the exhale releases my corruptive thoughts from my cerebral brain, corral the many voices in my head, the softer, focused, spirit side present and takes its place into the forefront, the primary focus. The multitude of purpose driven breaths I inhale, and exhale fill in voids, with a sense of satisfaction and fulfillment, I am complete, I am ready. I begin the first writing assignment and adventure in the workshop, Find & Amplify Your Voice.

As I open my eyes, an ear-to-ear smile forms on my face, I cannot help but feel the anticipation and awe of this moment, my mind raring to go. It is a magical moment when the world and all it is, changes to a wonderland and all that it can be. I grab a pen and paper and relish the possibilities with an eager heart, mind and soul and begin to tell the unique and unequivocally delightful story of me, Kent Deslongchamp and the Collective Crazy Colorful Christmas Cookie and Candy Celebration and Collaboration.

• • •

I was born under the crescent moon of a star filled winter Colorado sky at 11:36 pm at Rose Medical Center in Denver. From my first breath the fierceness of the Fire sign Sagittarius blazed into my soul, the desire to seek out adventures activated, and my presence, born unto this Earth, emanating endless energy, into a channeled connectedness, my powerful, plentiful personality and passionate persona permeating into every crevice, into every molecule, into everything for all time during the life I would live here on Earth. Being born near Christmas is probably the reason for the obsession behind my passion, starting with the spirit of the season filling my soul, and the euphoric kindred connection filling my heart and ending with the well wishes for peace, harmony, joy, and hope for all humankind filling the air. My birthday begins my holiday traditions and suave soirees, that yes, are oh so merry and oh so gay! In my travels during this holiday time, be they at a small guest house in Germany or grand villas in Italy, farms along the front range or cozy cottages in Canada, I savor the communion and participation in the plethora of Christmas cultures and holiday traditions, the comparing of local flavors, and the infusion of family recipes into my own, are just a few of the moments that make Christmas so incredible to me and fill me with jubilation and delightful exultation!

These core Christmas values are an intricate instilled part of me, easily rolling over into the realm of fabulous food. The collective collaboration of these ventured values, along with the felicity foods fabricate, infused with the cultural flavors, transcend into my exclusive, extraordinary month-long food festivity. This extravaganza is inspired by my collective Christmas cooking celebration created and crafted with: cookie baking, candy making, frosting topping, delightful decorating, spectacular sprinkle spreading, and a gaggle of glitter and glam galore, all hand-made and created with care and compassion. My basic holiday Christmas cookies are a mix of Chocolate Chip, Oatmeal Raisin, Peanut Butter, Gingerbread Men and Women, Sugar Cookies in shapes of Christmas Trees, Angels, Bells, Snowflakes and Snowmen. Then the candy varieties are added to include Marshmallow Rocky Road Chocolate Clusters, White Chocolate Toffee Peanut Clusters, Crushed Peppermint Candy Cane Crunch, Maraschino Cherry Chocolate Clusters, Butter Pecan and Almond Toffee, and White Chocolate Chip Health Crunch. Each cookie and candy is made and labored with love, the ingredients mixed forming the perfect amount of essence to fortuitous fellowships forming with those who feast upon the fabulousness of these flavors, and divulge in flamboyance of this part of the festivity, all enhancing this enthralling suave soiree and Christmas celebration.

Each and every aspect of these essential moments have been centered around food, fun and friendships. Now tis the time for shift in gear, the last leg of this festivity here. The season's spirit, harmony, and glee spark this next step. This truly is my favorite part, the heart and soul of what Christmas is all about, when it stops being the making and baking and all about me, I get to be just like Santa , something I simply adore, it is time for the giving of all the goodies as gifts galore. Boxes and bags filled to the brim , wrapped and decorated with ribbons, confetti, bows and colorful trim. I get so excited, and so it begins. Gifts gleefully given to family and friends, neighbors, co-workers, church goers, and bartends, bank tellers, marketplace sellers, gas station attends, cooks, wait staff, grocery baggers, bookkeepers, the trash folks and also street sweepers, bakers, barbers, beauticians, my coworkers too, strangers on the corners, delivery drivers stopping by, even unexpected guests who stop to say "hi." All get gifts with cookies and candy, ending this festivity in a finale that's dandy. So ring in the New Year about to start and *Auld Lang Syne* lest us not forget, good tidings to you and wishes bestowed with lots of cheer, until my next birthday of 64 year, when alas the Christmas cookies and candies will again appear.

~KENT DESLONGCHAMP

SESAME CHICKEN AND MY GRANDMOTHER

As a child, I was exposed to the food of different cultures. I remember in the 2nd or 3rd grade, we had a cultural event with foods from different cultures. While growing up, my mom was always a good sport in taking me to new restaurants and trying things alongside me at least once. I remember having fried plantains for the first time. I couldn't believe a banana could be prepared this way. Or the first time tasting the spice of kimchi and the tears that rolled down my cheeks from it burning, so good. I was floored at how the space differed from what I was used to with jalapenos and green chilies. I remember being at Costco and trying "exotic" jerkies like kangaroo from one of the samplers. I also remember the first time I had alligator and frog legs.

So when I say I'm a foodie. I really am....

But there is one dish that rocks my senses. Sesame Chicken with egg fried rice. I don't remember my first time eating this delish dish, but I do remember why I loved it. I love it because it reminds me of my grandmother, Mama Lela. It reminds me of her order that would always go with mine, Royal (Cashew) Chicken. This dish is much like my grandmother's; sweet and savory when prepared well. When my grandmother felt good, she was a kind woman with a sweet tooth, who knew how to laugh. She was complex, like the savory part of this dish, and knew how to stand her own ground.

Visually Sesame Chicken is stunning when served fresh and hot; I love the way you can see the steam wafting off.

Upon arrival at your table, it glistens and holds a warm amber color. My grandmother was someone who appreciated fashion. She was modest but knew how to glam up when the occasion arose. As she got older and sicker, that was something that was taken away from her. First, to go was her shoes. She loved shoes. Because of diabetes' effect on her feet and toes, she was left to wear, what I called ,Frankenstein boots (orthotic tennis shoes). Then her overall wardrobe was reduced to basic jogging suits. Something she could easily have the energy to put on and take off. Her personality used to glow and be warm like amber, but each time she got sick, her warmth would grow cooler and cooler, like leftovers expiring.

Even the smell of Sesame Chicken now takes me back to memories of her. She used to take me to the movies one-on-one, and we would grab Chinese food afterward. While writing this I just now noticed that I haven't been eating Sesame Chicken, the dish I still call my favorite, as much since she passed. That's going on 9 years now. I thought maybe my taste buds had changed, which could be true, but this dish was *our* dish. It was countless meals sitting, laughing, joking, and the occasional difference of opinion, Just BEing together. I miss that.

~SYDNEY JACKSON-CLOCKSTON

"KAMABOKO?"

My mom spent most of her childhood overseas. Her family lived in Japan and Hong Kong where they attended international schools. She and her sisters were exposed to so many cultures and people that many of us don't get to experience. She shared some of that culture with us through food. One of our very favorite dishes growing up was Somen Salad. She would prepare it the night before because, like many dishes, it was much better after the flavors had commingled for several hours. It was always prepared in the same dish, a gold Cinderella Pyrex casserole dish with a glass lid. As a child, it seemed to be so big that we, as children, were dwarfed by its size. And that was important because we devoured Somen Salad. My mom just couldn't make enough.

The dish got its name from Somen noodles, a wheat noodle, with a light saltiness that you could only find at an Asian market. They're rather delicate when cooked, and we found them very slurpable. Freshly cooked, they're light in color, but after marinating, the noodles take on the dark color of the dressing. The salad itself isn't complicated. It had a base of lettuce, iceberg as a child, but now I use romaine as an adult. Then there was an egg patty, cut into bite-sized pieces, green onion, ham, and the absolute best part, Kamaboko, a Japanese fish cake. It came mounted on a wood block, with white in the center and a bright pink layer on the outside. If you sliced it from the end, it looked a bit like a pink and white rainbow. This too was cut into bite sized pieces. It has a very mild taste, a bit umami (earthy and savory), and a chewy texture. My brother, sister, and I would sneak pieces whenever mom wasn't looking. And when possible, we'd sneak some noodles too. What child can resist noodles?

The dressing brought a complexity to an otherwise simple salad. Flavored with mushroom soy, tarragon vinegar, and sesame oil, it brought tang and depth to the salad. It was almost impossible to wait until the next day, but it was certainly worth it.

Mom was a big believer in not wasting food and eating everything on your plate. Sometimes, we could invite friends to join us for dinner. Since we loved this dish so much, we couldn't imagine anyone else not liking it. But children are picky, and I suppose as an adult, I can see how unusual this salad would be for children who hadn't been exposed to many different cultures. Egg in salad?? Weird. I don't actually remember what my friends thought of the salad, but I am so grateful we got to try new foods and flavors. Truly, my favorite foods from childhood are mostly from different cultures.

Over the years, as children grew up and moved away, we rarely had my mom's Somen salad. Mom stopped eating gluten and getting the right ingredients is quite a trek to the big city. Yet... It's still worth the trip to get the perfect ingredients. Even with ingredients that aren't quite from the original recipe, this salad brings back such great memories of family dinners. In fact, I have a block of Kamaboko sitting in my freezer... I just may have to stop at H-Mart on my way home from the workshop to pick up a few ingredients. It's high time to make a big batch of Somen Salad to share with those of us who can still eat gluten. Perhaps I'll make a couple of servings for Mom, without the noodles.

~TAMARA CRIBLEY

BUYING A NEW CAR
MOOD AND TONE WRITING EXERCISE

Understanding mood and tone in your writing is key to creating emotional buy-in from your readers. While the reader is on their reading journey, think about how you would like them to feel. Perhaps you would like for them to be delighted, maybe enraged, should they be afraid, or would you like for them to literally LOL (laugh out loud) to the words written on the page?

During our *Amplify Your Voice* writing workshop, we did a mood and tone writing exercise so our writers could clearly see how the same experience can feel different to the reader while keeping mood and tone in mind. Before moving on to the samples on the following pages, we encourage you to pause and give the *Mood and Tone Writing Exercise* a try for yourself. Notice the difference between your writing and that of the writers in this book. Feel free to share your writings with our author community on Heylo (https://heylo.group/write-and-publish).

MOOD AND TONE WRITING EXERCISE:

Experiment with different tones and moods. Write a paragraph conveying the same information but with varying tones—formal, conversational, and humorous. Observe how these choices impact the emotional resonance and reader experiences. This exercise provides a practical understanding of the intricate dance between tone and mood in shaping your writing voice.

SYDNEY JACKSON-CLOCKSTON

Sample 1: This is it! I finally have the money saved to buy my new baby. She really is a beaut'. Look at that color. I LOVE red. And those rims. Oh, how they glisten and gleam. So hypnotizing when they spin. The bucket seats fit my ass like a glove. AND ohhhhh, that new leather smell!

Sample 2: I have worked so hard to save for this new, used car. The salesman tried his best to get me to look at brand-new cars, never driven before, but I knew I needed to be practical with my choice. We spent time going over miles-per-gallon and safety features. I finally landed on this four-door Mazda with bucket leather seats. And it's red… flashier than I wanted, but it will do.

Sample 3: Ted had been to this dealership before. It always made him chuckle when he saw his goofy brother-in-law Stu at work. Stu had gained some baby weight during his sister's pregnancy. Oftentimes, Ted wondered if he had given birth too. Stu's work button-up had popped, exposing his white undershirt and he wore a lime green bow tie that always matched his socks. Stu tried to open the doors to Ted's would be the new but used Red Mazda, but he grabbed the wrong keys!

TAMARA CRIBLEY

Sample 1: As with so many things, a major purchase comes with loads of research and even more overthinking. This car… What do I need? What do I want? Am I willing to spend that much for the perks? Probably not. I'm frugal, but not cheap. I want great value. Can I negotiate it to get what I want for a price I'm willing to pay? It feels a bit like a game, this negotiation. But then there are the dealerships where I don't get to negotiate… and I feel a sense of injustice. Hmm…. Yep. I think I'm good with the car I have. This is much too much for today.

Sample 2: Justine set foot on the dealership lot. It was time to consider a new vehicle. She knew what she needed, and had her list of "perks" in hand. It felt like she'd only had a moment to step out of the car and straighten her clothes before a salesman began to approach from the far side of the lot. She glanced up and froze. Goodness! She wasn't ready for this kind of interaction. Why couldn't they let her take a moment to walk the lot and contemplate the different options? Quickly averting her eyes, Justine opened the driver's door and plopped in. She nearly caught her foot in the door in her haste to retreat. Maybe she should buy a car online. Yes, that might be just the ticket.

Sample 3: It's time to find the next great thing. A new car. Bright shiny paint, with the scent of "new car" filling the interior. The budget may not quite allow for the fanciest of features, but man, technology has come so far. It's almost like you don't need to be a good driver, the car has you covered. So many things that used to cause anxiety have been overcome through technology. Lane assist, auto braking, even parallel parking. How did one manage to get from place to place in the 90's without having panic attacks at every turn? I am so ready for this. Bring on the car payment! It's worth the peace of mind.

Sample 1: Walking around the lot, I spotted her. The car of my dreams!

"Can I take her for a ride?" I asked the sales person.

I was surprised when a feminine voice came seemingly from under the hood of the car.

"Yes, please. Take me for a ride."

My eyes grew wide as I looked at the sales person, an unasked question on my face. He stood there, hands in pockets, grinning impishly, and shrugged his shoulders.

Sample 2: The lot was nearly bare this time of year. Last year's models were nearly sold out, and the new year's models hadn't yet arrived.

"Would you like to test drive something?" Asked the sales person. "I can grab the keys to anything that catches your attention."

Nothing grabbed my attention.

"I'm not sure. Maybe I'll come back when you have more cars available."

Sample 3: The lot was nearly bare. There weren't many new cars to choose from. I didn't see any models from my list of potential cars that I had researched.

The sales person approached me, his face lit up with a bright smile.

"Good morning! Can I show you this model right here? This is my favorite car on the lot. She's a very under-appreciated automobile, but you get a lot of great features for a lot less than most models cost. She's a super smooth ride. Quiet. Very comfortable inside with a lot of legroom. And with today's gas prices, her gas mileage is easy on the wallet."

Maybe I had missed something in my research. I was excited to test drive this car. Let's grab those keys!

KENT DESLONGCHAMP

This exercise was so interesting. We each had the same subject—"Buying a car," and same prompt, write in three perspectives. I started and ended each perspective with the same line, and it was fascinating to go through the process in a short, timed period and see the outcome with choices to the mood, tone, and voice. It was so perplexing that none of us four writers came up with the same perspectives, or same choices, each unique just like each of us in the workshop. I really liked the discussion after seeing and hearing how each one of us came up with our idea, developed our idea then chose our style and wrote our assignment. My three perspectives were the nostalgic past and buying a car from family, and the emotional reaction to the process and the ease of the process today. All three stemmed from the interesting factor that my elderly parents were trying to buy a car, at that time. The perspective of the uncle car salesman is how my folks still see buying a car today. I have found that it is impossible to teach them anything about computers or on the computer, let alone about the automated computer process of buying a car, which is where the other two perspectives stemmed from. The emotional aspect, my frustration, their confusion, and the ease of computers today, obviously my own perspective. Thanks mom and dad for making this assignment a little bit easier than anticipated, however the actual process of buying a new car, not so much!

Sample 1: Today buying a car is vastly different than in the past. Why? Gone are the days of your uncle, dressed in that spiffy polyester bright colored suit, ready to show you that "beauty" that he picked out especially just for you, with that "special family discount" and all those "extras" that he is throwing in. The bantering and the bargaining trying to get that "special family discount "price reduced, those "extras" taken off, next that safety check, the kick of the tires and the oil level checked, perfect! Finally reaching a deal, only to go through the same bantering with the financing. After a long exhausting day with your uncle, you drive off the lot in your new car. Yes, buying a car is not what it used to be.

Sample 2: Today buying a car is vastly different than in the past. Today you do not have to deal with competitive salespeople, nor do you need to leave your house, you don't even need to get dressed if you don't want to. Everything is computerized from beginning to end. No human interaction, non-emotional, it is a direct, expediated process. Look at inventory, pictures of the car, pick out the car you want, pick out the options you desire, pick out your financing, pick out whether delivery or pick up, hit the submit button and you have a new car. You can even get your grocery shopping completed, and buy jeans on sale at the same time, too. Yes, buying a buying a car today is not what it used to be.

Sample 3: Today buying a car is vastly different than in the past. Buying a car online terrifies me. How can you trust the person you're buying from? How do you know if the car is even real? How do you know if the whole thing is real or if you're getting ghosted? I don't even know what that means. How do you even know if you're looking at something real? All the choices, all the options, all the forms to fill out, all online and all on the computer, it's all very confusing. Then the financial stuff, putting your info on the internet. How do you keep from getting taken with so many scams? I get so worked up, blood pressure goes up, I get stressed out and I freeze up and I can't even think and must stop. I have yet to buy a car online and probably never will. Yes, buying a car today is not what it used to be.

CHOOSE YOUR OWN PROMPT

Even the most experienced authors benefit from challenging themselves with writing prompts that are outside of their typical scope of work. So as a new writer finding and developing your writing voice, taking on a writing prompt challenge is an excellent way to spark creativity and warm up for a productive writing session. *Pro tip: If you ever feel writer's block, writing prompts are a great way to get out of your own head and write just for fun.*

During our *Amplify Your Voice* workshop, we sent folks home with several prompts they could dig into for homework. Feel free to take the same prompts and have fun writing your own samples. Our community of authors would love to read your take on one or more of the challenges. Sharing your writing with others is that healthy risk that just may push you into self-publishing your own work. Join our community on Heylo (https://heylo.group/write-and-publish). Don't worry about perfection just start writing.

WRITING WARM-UP PROMPT EXERCISE:

Selecting a writing prompt is a crucial step for new writers, as it can spark creativity and set the tone for a productive writing session. Don't worry about perfection just start writing.

Pick one of the following prompts for tonight's homework and bring it to tomorrow's class.

Word Prompt

Write a short story or poem inspired by the word "whisper." Explore how the concept of whispers can shape the narrative and evoke emotions.

Visual Prompt:

Describe a scene based on an image of an abandoned, overgrown garden. Consider the emotions, memories, or stories this visual prompt might elicit.

Dialogue Prompt:

Start a conversation between two characters who meet unexpectedly on a train. Explore their backgrounds, motivations, and the impact of this chance encounter on their lives.

Genre Twist:

Take a genre you've never tried before, such as science fiction, and write a short story incorporating elements of the genre. How does this new setting impact your storytelling?

Personal Reflection:

Reflect on a vivid childhood memory involving water. Describe the sensations, emotions, and the impact of this memory on your present self.

Character Exploration:

Create a character who possesses an unusual ability, such as the power to manipulate time. Explore how this ability influences their relationships and choices.

Conflict Resolution:
Write a scene where two characters who have been estranged for years must come together to resolve a long-standing conflict. Explore the emotions and challenges they face.

Setting Challenge:
Set a story entirely in an elevator. Explore the dynamics between characters, the reasons for their presence, and the unfolding events within this confined space.

Unexpected Twist:
Start a story with the line, "The letter arrived, and everything changed." Explore the unexpected consequences and revelations that follow the receipt of this mysterious letter.

Flash Fiction Challenge:
Write a complete story in 100 words or less about a character who discovers a hidden door in their home. What lies beyond, and what impact does it have on their life?

Time Travel Dilemma:
Your character discovers a device that allows them to travel in time but only for a single day. Explore the choices they make and the consequences of altering a pivotal moment.

Inanimate Object Perspective:
Write a story from the perspective of an inanimate object, like a key or a book. Explore the object's history, experiences, and the significance it holds for different characters.

Parallel Universes:

Explore a scenario where your character stumbles upon a portal to a parallel universe. Describe the differences between the two worlds and the challenges your character faces.

Nature's Influence:

Write a piece inspired by the changing seasons. Explore how nature's transformations mirror the emotions or experiences of the characters in your story.

WE ARE GOING TO PARTY LIKE IT'S 1999

CONFLICT RESOLUTION:

Write a scene where two characters who have been estranged for years must come together to resolve a long-standing conflict. Explore the emotions and challenges they face.

KENT DESLONGCHAMP

My thoughts and the take-aways, tools and learned processes for this assignment.

First thoughts: This was our first assignment in class, the first time actually writing on the spot and without preparation. I had to first gather my thoughts, to pick which prompt stood out and then begin. The whole project was only about 15 minutes from start to finish, so little time in preparing, categorizing, collaborating, writing, editing, closing and then sharing. The whole 15 minutes zoomed by. I never even got to the body of my story let alone the *Conflict Resolution*, thus not really doing a good job in reaching the goal of th is exercise. However, I learned a few things, had some takeaways and insights, and gathered new skills in this practice which enhanced the ideology behind the art of writing a short story.

What I learned: From the feedback of others, I learned that my style was very descriptive. I learned my writing takes the reader down a very visually, picturesque and detailed journey. My imagery and distinct, defined and detailed descriptions left little to the imagination. This style created and made easy to picture in ones mind, to imagine a character, setting, or the environment and even in the finite details. I learned that my focused words complimented my writing rather than just making it busy or being added without context. The focused detailed imagery hooked the reader and enticed the need and want for more. The characters were seen as real, instilling personality and a bond or closeness to them. The depth and emotional subcontext portrayed and expressed by distinct traits and characteristics depicting their emotional and mental state of being.

Things that need work: Things that were stated that needed some attention and practice to gain knowledge and skill set. My pace needed work, so I planned on setting a timer, practicing writing 5 minute timed writing tasks using the other prompts from this exercise. This would allow me as a writer to get a better understanding and defined feel for that period of time. My time management was seen as too meandering, not focused. I discovered that I spent a lot of time, thinking of and storyboarding the details, and in the telling of my story incorporating the details into my writing style and choices. It was understood that some readers do not want to wait for the end, don't want to have emotional context or history of the character, they desire or want the next, now. No sugar coating just plain and simple. I also, understand that readers with this reading belief, may not be jumping over to the Kent Page to find a book to read or to purchase, very often. This too turned into a lesson of knowing who I was, making no compromises and in being confident and articulate in telling compelling stories that people could relate to. Keeping true to my in my distinct descriptive and visually astute style and delivery was more important than to give up my writing distinctions, compromising my values with the possibility of those changes not even being of benefit to me or those true readers that hoped for this style and distinct writing from me, will ask for it, desire it and gladly purchase it for their reading pleasure conducive with their reading needs.

Thoughtful Storytelling: I spent a lot of time in the storyboarding stage, allowing for every single tiny minute thought or idea to flow freely and without interruption. I like to have choices, the more choices the better for me. This stage is my way of clearing out my mind, like having an Etch-A-Sketch brain putting everything on your mind down. Then picking it up, shaking it and clearing the slate blank to be filled by you, choosing what fits for this particular writing project. If I have suddenly lost my thought or find myself staring at a blank page, I can go back and look at the grand scheme of things, the big picture. This methodology then allows me to see things differently, more dynamic and in doing so, gain a broader perspective, which then allows for my thoughts to flow more freely and less confined. This is a great way of bringing about a fresh possibility to create an idea that the story did not have previously, the freedom to break away from a storyline that is blocked and stagnate, redirect intent, or find alternative reasoning. This is the process in this piece that I used and why I did not finish the assignment. I was stuck and went back to the page with my ideas, 1999 was written down which sparked "new millennial" which sparked the story line and the supporting content, the idea for the take away and call back. This the gave me the hook, which I intended to put next into the story, but I ran out of time and we moved on to the next discussion and assignment

• • •

I sat in my worn brown leather recliner, holding the large coffee mug in my hand, that read, *Nothing is impossible.* I had not really used this coffee mug, which had sat in the back of the cupboard, hidden behind the newer and familiar daily coffee mugs for years. There was a crack in the mug that separated the two s's in the word impossible, I sat looking at the crack in the mug, lost in my thoughts. The crack was jagged, like the icon used today for a lightning bolt. It stopped short of the top of the mug, but the crack wrapped around the mug, like a spiral before dissipating into the bottom of the mug. The crack in the mug was almost a mirror image of the moment in time when it was made in the mug…I paused, and thought to myself, *How long had it been since that day when it happened? When was the last time I saw Enrique? The preparator of that crack in the mug…Ah, yes, it was 1998, no, no. Ah yes, 1999. Just like the Prince song of that era.* That was the year that my life changed, rearranged and never to be the same. A moment that I thought could never be forgotten, yet here I was, struggling to remember the date today. I thought to myself, *My, how time flies. As I get older, memories can be erased and forgotten, even the most complicated, emotional and intense memories like the moment when the crack happened. Strange how memories can be whisked away, cleared from our minds, as if cobwebs growing in a doorway corner that are cleaned with a broom and then gone, as if it were never there before.*

The doorbell gave off its electronic ring, and the Nest camera opened to show me who was standing on the front porch, waiting to enter my home. Everything is electronic today. Your doorbell equipped with alarms and a camera, your watch which is now your phone, like Agent 99 from the TV series *Get Smart*, your car has keyless ignition, which is nothing like popping the clutch while being pushed to get it started. Even the appliances are all pre-programmed, like the cartoon series *The Jetsons*. All designed to make life easier, so they say. But for me, just figuring out how to turn anything on or off or use is so complicated and run by an application which you get from the internet and must download and program and have enough memory... Even something as simple as a light switch that with a flick of the finger in my day, turned on or off, today is automated, programmed and can have multi functions which slowly fade in to turn on, no instantaneous bright light. There are even settings to change the mood, the warmth of the room, programmed sequences for your daily scheduled events, waking up, going to bed, taking a piss. They even have a vast spectrum of colors to choose from that, without moving a single inch, can fade in or out and turn on or off, voice activated or pre-programmed, all on its own. Boy, things have sure changed, nothing is like the good old days, and looking at Enrique on the Nest camera, neither was he.

I stared at the image on the screen, where there was once a full head of curly brown, long luscious hair was now a shaved head with the glare of the front porch lights beaming off it. The muscular, solid worked out body was now plump and even a bit heavy. The brilliant smile that I used to see every day, was no where on this face, which was wrinkled, and the lips pursed and tense. Even the clothes which used to be so brilliant and colorful were earth toned and drab. The freshly pressed pants and starched shirts of yesteryear were now wrinkled and worn. This Enrique was vastly different from the Enrique that I had known and loved so long ago. I am sure he thought the same of me. Which, we will soon find out, if I would stop reminiscing and just open the damn door. I pushed the automated buzzer for the front door, smiling to myself, and even smirked, I don't even have to open the door to let someone in today. Enrique entered the room, and without a single second in time, whooshed back to that night, December 31, 1999. The night of a new millennium.

THE DOOR IN THE FLOOR

FLASH FICTION CHALLENGE:

Write a complete story in 100 words or less about a character who discovers a hidden door in their home. What lies beyond, and what impact does it have on their life?

SYDNEY JACKSON-CLOCKSTON

Writing this piece was a challenge because I could only use 100 words! What I learned by taking on this prompt is that sometimes you have to write more to get your ideas out on the page and then edit down to meet your goal or, in this case, challenge. I literally had to write a backstory that came to 1500 words. This allowed me enough materials to determine what to include and exclude to paint a vivid picture and pack a punch for my audience.

Oftentimes in writing, you have to write more or several scenarios just to go back and edit them down. For new writers, this can be frustrating, but it's part of the process.

• • •

Maloney started skimming the floor and noticed a scuff mark pattern by the workbench. She moved the bench and discovered a door! How could there be a door, and where did it go? She opened the door, and there were stairs leading downward into the dark.

Pulling out her cellphone flashlight Maloney started her descent. At the bottom, she flipped a switch, and the lights flickered on. In the middle of the room, tied up to a beam and clearly beaten, were the two tourists who had gone missing.

Her mind started to race. Who were her parents?

WHO AM I? WHO AM I MEANT TO BE?

INANIMATE OBJECT PERSPECTIVE:

Write a story from the perspective of an inanimate object, like a key or a book. Explore the object's history, experiences, and the significance it holds for different characters.

TONYA ROCHE

The prompt I used was "Inanimate Object Perspective". I was intrigued by the idea of showing emotion through an inanimate object. I challenged myself to make the experience "believable" without being too outlandish.

Thinking through the five senses, I immediately ruled out the idea of using "taste" and "smell" to draw in the reader's experience. How would a piece of rock taste or smell? It could be done, I suppose, but I wanted this piece to feel realistic, to defy logic.

I focused on the other three senses. Everything has a surface. A sort of skin. So, "feel" wasn't entirely far-fetched. I imagined how a rock might feel in its environment before and after excavating. I set out to describe as much of this experience as possible. This would be my most prominent sense, and I needed to extort it.

For "sight", I tried to imagine what I might sense if I were blind. I closed my eyes and imagined sunshine. I closed my eyes and imagined beauty without details, ignoring my predetermined encyclopedia of memories.

I recalled watching deaf friends and colleagues "experi-
ence" sound through vibrations, and I tried to convey something
similar in my short story. I optimistically tried to come close
to capturing these emotions, and hopefully I succeeded. Enjoy
the story.

• • •

I lie here, deep in the plateaus of Madagascar, buried in my cold, damp tomb. Many centuries I have waited for my release, noting the passing of time as the sun drifts overhead, warming my face before dipping below the horizon, and casting my world into cool shadow. Aware, again, of the cycles of the moon as it moves from dark to light and dark, again.

Tides wash over me and then recede, dancing in the arms of the changing seasons. Water flows over me. Washing me clean. Smoothing my rough edges. I know my purpose in this life, but my form is yet to be revealed.

The Gods have blessed me this day, for I am discovered. Hands, weathered by years of hard work, gently lift me from my ancient grave, exposing me fully to the hot Madagascar sun. I loosen a silent sigh of ecstasy as my whole being is warmed, as though folded into a loving embrace. My veins pulse as though alive. Indeed, I feel alive for the first time since the north wind whispered the announcement of the birth of a messiah. A sense of a long-awaited adventure excites and frightens me at the same time.

Softness cradles and protects my fragile body. I am joined by others who have also been liberated from the stone burrows that entrapped them. All aware of our destinies from the beginning of our existence. We travel in silence, relishing in the new sensations, aware of motion never before experienced.

We listen to the soothing hums of machines; feel the sway of the ocean waves. We are all connected in a way that needs no communication. We each feel the other, and we are comforted by the familiar intimacy.

The journey is long, but it is nothing compared to the lifetime of waiting for this very moment.

We are all excited, and a little anxious. The unknown is always frightening. There is comfort in the familiar, even when the familiar is oppressive. But we are here, now, and the familiar is forever left behind us.

Things happen quickly. So many sensations and experiences I have never known. New. Exciting. Unpleasant at times, but even the unpleasantness is endured, as I know it is the way to greater things.

Finally, my transformation is complete. I feel my new form. I am sleek and beautiful. Truly a work of art. I see the look of admiration when eyes fall upon me. Pride fills my stone heart, and I know I am ready to fulfill my purpose.

Opening my heart and my mind, I summon the energy of the earth. I draw it in like breath. Sweet, emerald light fills my core. Life. Happiness. The power of creativity. Protection. I pull the energy in until I am full, and then, I rest. And wait.

Soon. I can feel it in my jasper bones.

I chance a vain peek at my reflection in the shiny surface in my new domain. If fate had graced me with the ability to weep, my crystal tusks would have been wet from my tears. I am more beautiful than I could ever have imagined. My heart rejoices.

Armed with the knowledge of my sacred purpose, and my identity finally revealed, I mentally reach out for the one who was meant to be mine. My true spiritual match.

When she finds me, we both know I was created especially for her and for her alone. She gathers me gingerly and holds me to her bosom.

She whispers, "You are the one. You called to me, and I have found you."

We both feel the instant connection. I know what she needs, and together, we will create something wonderful and uniquely ours. She is my heart, and I am hers.

Her little jasper elephant.

IT'S LIKE A RALLY CROSS COARSE...

NATURE'S INFLUENCE:

Write a piece inspired by the changing seasons. Explore how nature's transformations mirror the emotions or experiences of the characters in your story.

TAMARA CRIBLEY

I have a tendency to write about things that take up space in my daily life. This prompt immediately called to me. While I love winter, I also loathe it. And this was just the prompt to start exploring that conflicted relationship. Though I didn't quite reach a conclusion, this was an exercise that allowed me to explore the duality of my feelings for the season.

• • •

It's like a rally cross course, my driveway. Two and a half miles from the mailbox to the house, with the last mile being privately maintained. And in the summer, when the road is dry and relatively flat, we barely pay it any attention. Sure, the washboard texture that can rattle your brain may draw some ire, but living in the country, it's something you get used to. My vehicles are always dusty. To the garage-parking urbanite, it looks like I don't care much about the maintenance of my vehicle, but alas... it's a compromise I'm happy to make to live with beautiful views, fresh air, and solitude.

Winter. That's another story. I once loved to watch the snow fall silently through the night, blanketing the landscape. The more, the better. There's nothing quite like sitting in front the of wood burning stove, pup curled at my side, Attired in the cutest darn pajama set with cozy slippers, we sit with a fluffy blanket draped across us both. I'd read, or maybe sit in silence, contemplating life and just being present. For the first year or so, I loved the snow, and the inconvenience went largely dismissed.

But snow, especially in large amounts, on roads that aren't maintained like we expect in the city, can be… frustrating. Three-foot drifts can make the road impassible. Heck, in a car, a foot of snow might mean you're trapped until you and the neighbors can get the heavy equipment out to clear the road. And when you have somewhere to be, first thing in the morning, well, you might be late. And it's not always you. Sometimes, a neighbor has attempted the trek, and gotten stuck… trapped in deep snow, with no easy way to pass them. The neighborly thing to do, is to help. So you do, even though it makes you late. But that's okay too. I don't mind stopping to help. I've been on the receiving end of that help too. It's a beautiful thing to have neighbors you can count on when things get tough, away from fast resources.

It's the mud, after the big snow, that makes my eye start to twitch and my teeth grind. We need the moisture. I keep telling myself, we NEED the moisture. But the mud… oh, the mud. After some storms, it's so deep, and thick and sticky, that I can't get the car to the house. And then it's a call for help, or I'm slogging a mile through shin deep, clay-infused mud… an effort that feels nearly impossible.

By the time you reach the house and figure out how to remove the muddy shoes and winter layers, so that you don't track it into the house, you're exhausted. You just want to collapse on the couch and vent your frustrations. Somehow the mud seems to last longer than the snow.

But it's a mixed bag. The weather plays with your heart, your need for sunshine, vitamin D, and warm weather. The mud only arrives as the weather gets warmer. The temperature may still be on the chilly side, but the radiant heat of the bright sun melts the snow. Sometimes slowly, ensuring that the mud will persists.... It feels like it's indefinite, but maybe it's only for the next week. Or on a warm day, the mild temperatures and radiant heat, melt it all in one fell swoop, creating the everlasting mud pit that we must somehow figure out how to navigate... Are you ready for the rally course? There's no slowing down, for fear of getting trapped. You can't help but slide through corners, drifting from one side of the road to the other. And be sure to miss that hole. The last time you dropped into it, your brain rattled. Fortunately, the road is straight, and the hazards limited; no trees to jump in front of you.

I'm ready for warm weather, sunny skies, and a little less of a challenging trek home.

AN INVITATION TO FIND & AMPLIFY *YOUR* VOICE

Six. That's the number of times I have started rewriting on this idea. There's so much I want to say about the drive to write. But when I free write, I can get caught in the weeds, running down a rabbit hole, finding myself in vastly different territory than where I started. It's a bit like when I get into philosophical conversations with people. I may not have a clear point, at least not in the beginning. I have to work through and process it to clarify and calcify my thoughts. Sometimes it's the process of asking questions. Other times, its hearing the ideas as they initially present and then checking them for authenticity and how they resonate with my true values. It's an exploration of the difference between my gut reaction and the more considered version of what I really think or feel. My good friend and co-host, Sydney, uses the analogy that we are either microwave or crockpot thinkers. I am definitely a crockpot. Whether in conversation or writing, my thoughts often don't become clear until I have examined them six ways from Sunday. It's the reason I get so frustrated in an argument or when I find myself put on the spot to defend an idea or value, without having the time to prepare for it. I am a 'muller.' I process ideas over time. I test them for efficacy and validity. I analyze them from every angle and consider opposing viewpoints. It is through this process that I find my true voice. It is one of the reasons that I place such a high value on the written word.

Nearly as important as sharing one's true voice, is the ability to 'speak,' uninterrupted. In the written word, you can say exactly what you think or mean, without interjections or disruptions. No one can derail your train of thought because it is already *ink on the page*, so to speak. It is the reason that self-publishing holds such an important place in our society and underrepresented communities. We repress voices for so many reasons. They might be unpopular, uncomfortable, different, or just… very quiet. Collectively, we seem to amplify just a few voices, more for their function of increasing engagement than for merit or value. They gain traction and overshadow so very many worthy voices. For me, self-publishing gives people a voice. It amplifies it. It is a platform that begins to level the playing field. It is, at some level, accessible to most people. It also becomes more important than ever to publish with intention—to define goals and publish in a manner that resonates with *your* audience. To create an experience where *your* message can be received.

The majority of what I read is fiction. It serves many functions for me. It is an escape from reality, an exploration of different worlds, cultures, and lifestyles. It is a glimpse into the lives and experiences of others, that teach me empathy and compassion for lives, different from my own. It is a sense of companionship that my experiences and feelings aren't unique. That I am not isolated in my highs and lows. We are more alike than we are different. There is a vulnerability that is somehow easier to express in a story than it is on your Facebook page. It is a legacy, written and recorded.

Whether you write fiction or non-fiction, a story for children, or one that hope helps people cope through difficult times, your voice matters. It is worthy of being heard.

This is the power of self-publishing. But there is so much more to being heard than just getting words down on a page. Finding your voice is about more than the content you want to share. It is a journey of discovery. It is about understanding who your audience is and how you can reach them so that they are receptive to your message. It demands that you set goals, both for writing and publishing, so that you can find the right path to achieve them.

I am so proud of the writers who are featured in this edition of *The Nudge to Write*. Within a short period, just two weekends, they have demonstrated an evolution of their voice and intent. There is clarity that has made itself present and which demands attention. Their voices *will* be heard, their messages clear for those who are intended to receive them. It is an honor to help them in their journey to become published authors.

I invite you to do the same. Whether you're just starting to discover your voice, or you have been on this path for many years, contemplating how to reach your audience, you are welcome in this community. Join us on Heylo (https://heylo.group/write-and-publish). Share your writing, ask questions, and support your fellow writers. When you're ready, join us for a workshop. We'd be honored to help you become a published author.

To Tonya and Kent, thank you for taking part in this workshop. I have been so inspired by you, and your writing. As I sat at my desk, typesetting this book, I read every single essay aloud. Each of you has a unique voice, with a powerful purpose. I cannot wait to see the mark you make on the world.

Tamara Cribley
Owner of The Deliberate Page, LLC

For more information about the
*Find & Amplify Your Voice Writing
Workshops*, visit

www.DeliberatePage.com/Workshops

www.ingramcontent.com/pod-product-compliance
Lightning Source LLC
Chambersburg PA
CBHW030252270626
47156CB00021B/1746